# The Virginia Reckless Driving Handbook

## A Driver's Guide to Avoiding
## This Serious Criminal Conviction

**Luke J. Nichols, Esq.**

**For questions and comments, contact:**

Luke J. Nichols at
Nichols & Green pllc
Fairfax, Va.
(703) 383-9222 (ph)
(703) 383-9220 (fx)
lnichols@nicholsgreen.com
www.nicholsgreen.com

**ISBN: 978-0-9828928-3-1**

**Spectrum Publishing**
**Fairfax, VA**

# Table of Contents

# Introduction

Reckless driving is one of the most underestimated criminal charges in Virginia. Too many people think that reckless driving is just a fancy traffic ticket. It is not.

Reckless driving is a serious criminal charge. It is a class 1 misdemeanor, which is the most serious misdemeanor in Virginia. Other class 1 misdemeanors include assault and battery, driving under the influence (DUI), and possession of a concealed weapon.

Reckless driving carries a sentence of up to 12 months in jail and a six-month driver's license suspension (two years for racing). A reckless driving conviction can cost a driver up to $2,500 in fines in addition to court costs, Department of Motor Vehicle (DMV) fees, and massive insurance premium hikes.

A reckless driving conviction has severe affects for a driver's auto insurance, especially if that driver has a good driving record. A single reckless driving conviction may double a driver's insurance premiums for the next three to five years.

Drivers can also lose their job if they drive for work or require security clearance. People convicted of reckless driving may be forced to disclose their conviction on background checks, job applications, and applications for higher education. In some cases reckless driving can prevent military enlistment or admission to practice law.

A reckless driving conviction cannot be expunged. Once you have been convicted for reckless driving in Virginia, it is on your criminal record forever. Expungements are only available if the charges are dismissed or dropped.

A conviction for reckless driving is also a six-demerit-point violation in Virginia, and it remains on the driving record for eleven years. If a driver has a less than perfect driving record, that driver may be in jeopardy of having their license revoked by the DMV or being placed on driving probation in addition to any court suspensions. DMV probation or suspension will be automatic for minors if they are convicted of reckless driving.

Having a reckless driving conviction on your driving record also means that police will be less likely to give you warnings for simple traffic violations and judges will be harsher in the future.

Reckless driving is a very serious charge; however, the good news is that there is a lot that can be done to prevent the severe consequences of conviction. An effective attorney can help a driver with literally dozens of defenses and possible alternatives to conviction.

The purpose of this book is to educate drivers about reckless driving in order to empower them to find and utilize the best reckless driving attorneys. If you have been charged with reckless driving then you need to read this book.

# Chapter 1:
## "What Is Reckless Driving?"
A Description of the Laws Related to
Reckless Driving in Virginia

**Reckless Driving Is Complicated**

Reckless driving can be complicated and confusing. There are 14 ways to be convicted of reckless driving, and there are less severe non-reckless versions of each of these forms of reckless driving. Consequently, two drivers who make the same mistake may be charged with two different crimes.

For example, a driver pulled over for driving 82 miles per hour (mph) in a 65 mph zone can be charged with reckless driving or, instead, can be given a simple speeding ticket. Furthermore, a person charged with reckless driving for passing a school bus (Va. Code §46.2-859) could have been issued a simple traffic citation for passing a stopped school bus (Va. Code § 46.2-844).

Whether a driver receives a traffic ticket or is issued a summons for reckless driving has everything to do with the officer who pulls over the driver and the circumstances surrounding the offense. Some law enforcement departments have hard and fast rules about when an officer must and must not issue a summons for reckless driving.

For example, in Northern Virginia, local police will often write speeding tickets for driving 76 mph in a 55 mph zone, but the state troopers on the same highway usually issue summons for reckless driving.

The specific circumstances also affect whether a person is charged with reckless driving versus a simple traffic violation. A poor driving record, having a child in the car, irritating the police officer, causing or nearly causing an accident and other similar circumstances are examples of things that may cause a law enforcement officer to write a summons for reckless driving instead of a simple traffic ticket.

## The 14 Types of Reckless Driving

The following sections discuss the many ways a driver can be convicted for reckless driving.

### Va. Code §46.2-862(i) & (ii): Reckless by Speed

A driver can be convicted for reckless driving by either 1) going 20 mph over the speed limit **or** 2) driving over 80 mph. Therefore, a person driving 35 mph in a 15 mph zone is guilty of reckless driving, and a person driving 81 mph in a 70 mph zone is also guilty of reckless driving.

### Va. Code § 46.2-861: Reckless by Excessive Speed for the Conditions

Driving at or below the speed limit can also be considered reckless driving if the road conditions are not safe enough for that speed. For example, a person driving 65 mph in a 65 mph zone during a snow storm or heavy rain could be charged with reckless driving if the road conditions are not safe enough for that speed.

### Va. Code § 46.2-852: Reckless Driving General Rule

Driving on a public road in a way that endangers anyone's "life, limb, or property" can be reckless driving. This statute is a catch-all for any unsafe driving practices, such as driving the wrong way down a one-way street, falling asleep at the wheel, backing up on a highway, and other similar practices. The most common application of this statute is in accident cases.

This statute is also sometimes issued in situations where an officer believes a person is driving drunk but there is not sufficient evidence to charge DUI.

### Va. Code § 46.2-864: Reckless on Private Property

This statute covers driving that endangers "life, limb or property" on private property open to the public or on public roads under construction. The most common examples involve parking lots.

### Va. Code §46.2-859: Reckless by Passing a School Bus

Passing a school bus that is equipped with warning signs and flashing lights while it is stopped to load or unload passengers is considered reckless driving. The driver must remain stopped until the passengers are all clear of the road or until the bus starts moving. This rule does not apply if there is a physical barrier separating the driver's lane from the school bus.

### Va. Code § 46.2-853: Reckless by Improper Control/Faulty Brakes

Driving a vehicle that is not under proper control or has faulty brakes is considered reckless driving. If a driver tells a police officer that the accident occurred because the car's brakes, steering, or any other mechanism failed, that driver runs the risk of being charged with reckless driving. It is a defense to this type of reckless driving to argue that the driver did not have notice that there was a problem with the car prior to the incident.

## Va. Code § 46.2-855: Reckless by Driving with Impaired Control/View Because of Passengers

Driving while passengers obstruct the driver's front or side view, or impair the driver's ability to operate the vehicle, is reckless driving. Sometimes, law enforcement officers incorrectly charge drivers with this form of reckless driving when there are more passengers than seat belts in the front seat regardless of whether the driver's view or operation was actually obstructed.

## Va. Code § 46.2-854: Reckless by Passing on a Curve

Passing a car on the crest of hill, on a curve, or anywhere with an obstructed view of oncoming traffic is reckless driving.

## Va. Code §46.2-856: Reckless by Passing Two Vehicles Abreast

Reckless driving can also include passing two vehicles at the same time by driving on the shoulder or in the on-coming traffic lane(s) on a highway with two or more lanes of traffic in each direction.

## Va. Code § 46.2-857: Reckless by Driving Two Abreast in a Single Lane

It is considered reckless driving for two vehicles (other than bikes, motorcycles, or similar vehicles) to travel in the same lane, or for one vehicle to pass another without completely leaving the original lane.

## Va. Code § 46.2-858: Reckless by Passing at a Railroad or Pedestrian Crossing

If a driver passes another vehicle at a railroad crossing or while a pedestrian is crossing in front of the passed vehicle, the driver may be charged with reckless driving. There is an exception to this rule if there are multiple lanes dedicated for passing or if the road is marked for passing with a dashed yellow line.

## Va. Code § 46.2-860: Reckless by Failing to Signal

It is considered reckless driving to turn, slow down, or stop without giving a proper signal. When turning, the driver must continuously signal for 50 feet before turning if the posted speed limit is 35 mph or less. Otherwise, the driver must signal for 100 feet.

## Va. Code § 46.2-863: Reckless by Failure to Yield

Reckless driving also includes cutting off a vehicle on a highway when entering from a side road. If a driver enters a highway from a side road without a yield sign the driver 1) must come to a stop before entering the highway, and 2) must not pull in front of a vehicle that is less than 500 feet away.

## Va. Code § 46.2-865: Reckless by Racing

Racing vehicles on public property at any time or on private property open to the public (such as parking lots) without permission is reckless driving. Racing also comes with an elevated punishment that includes suspension of the driver's license for at least six months and up to two years.

**Related Lesser Offenses**

Va. Code § 46.2-870: Speeding

The prosecution (or occasionally the judge) may amend the charge of reckless driving (46.2-862) to speeding. Speeding carries a maximum fine of $250 (plus $62 in court costs) and is not a criminal charge. However, speeding over 20 mph over the limit has the same effects on insurance as reckless driving and also carries six demerit points which can lead to a DMV administrative suspension if the driver has a bad driving record. Speeding stays on your Virginia DMV record for five years.

Va. Code § 46.2-869: Improper Driving

At the discretion of the prosecutor or judge, reckless driving may be reduced to improper driving, which is a traffic violation and not a criminal charge. The maximum fine for improper driving is $500 (plus $62 in court costs); however, improper driving has much less severe effects on insurance and carries only three demerit points that stay on your record for only three years.

Va. Code § 46.2-830: Failure to Obey a Highway Sign

This statute may be used any time a driver disobeys a highway sign. This can include speeding, driving the wrong way on a one-way road, an illegal u-turn, etc. Failure to obey a highway sign is a traffic infraction, has a maximum fine of $250, is only three DMV demerit points, and stays on a your record for only three years.

# Chapter 2:
## "How Bad Is It?"
### The Costs and Consequences of Conviction

## Reckless Driving Is a Serious Criminal Conviction

Most people do not realize until it is too late that reckless driving is a criminal charge, not a traffic infraction. Reckless driving is a class 1 misdemeanor. Other class 1 misdemeanors include DUI, assault, possession of marijuana, and petty larceny.

Like all class 1 misdemeanors, reckless driving can result in up to 12 months of jail time. However, the consequences of a reckless driving conviction can have far-reaching consequences that go beyond jail time.

## License Suspension

The court may suspend a driver's license for up to six months (two years for racing). This suspension takes effect immediately upon conviction, and the bailiff will confiscate the driver's license in the courtroom. Driving after suspension is a serious crime and carries penalties of up to 12 months in jail, additional license suspension, vehicle impound, and serious fines.

## Fines and Fees

A driver convicted of reckless driving may have to pay thousands in fines, higher insurance premiums, court fees, and DMV charges. Reckless driving carries a maximum fine of $2,500. In addition to a steep fine, drivers convicted of reckless driving may have to pay $62 in court costs and a $175 DMV license reinstatement fee. Applicants for a restricted driver's license may also face a $220 restricted license fee (*These fees change regularly; consequently, the dollar amounts in this book should be used as approximations only*).

## Expensive Insurance Premiums

Some insurance companies treat reckless driving the same as a first-time DUI. A single reckless driving conviction may double your insurance rates for three to five years. A driver convicted of reckless driving may pay $1,500 or more in extra insurance premiums because of the conviction. A reckless driving conviction can affect life and health insurance premiums as well.

## Criminal Record

Because reckless driving is a crime, it will remain on your permanent criminal record and cannot be expunged unless the charges are dismissed or dropped. A reckless driving conviction can prevent a law student from practicing law, disqualify a person for military service, jeopardize security clearance, and make finding a job harder. Reckless driving charges can blacklist a driver from many jobs that require employees to drive because of the extreme cost of insuring those with a reckless driving conviction and because of the employer's fear of being sued. Whether you are a truck driver, in-house nurse's assistant, delivery man, or construction laborer, a reckless driving conviction may affect your ability to get and keep a job.

## DMV License Suspension and Demerit Points

When Virginia drivers receive their license, they start with zero points on their driving record. Each year, they get +1 point on their driving record until they have a maximum of +5 points. If a driver is convicted of reckless driving, he will lose six points from his driving record and the conviction will remain on his driving record for eleven years (though the conviction will remain on his criminal record forever).

The Virginia DMV can suspend a Virginian driver's license, require the driver to take driver improvement classes, or place him on probation for excessive demerit points. This suspension is independent from the court's suspension, and the court cannot control the DMV's suspension.

For minors, any demerit point conviction means the driver must attend a driver improvement class. Failure to do so within 90 days results in a license suspension until the program is completed. A second point-conviction results in a 90-day license suspension. A third will result in a suspension for one year or until the offender reaches age 18, whichever is longer.

| Consequences of Demerit Points in Virginia (Adult Drivers) | | |
|---|---|---|
| | Within 12 months | Within 24 months |
| 8 points | Letter from DMV | Nothing |
| 12 points | Mandatory driver improvement class | Letter from DMV |
| 18 points | Mandatory 90-day license suspension + driver improvement class + probation for six months | Mandatory driver improvement class |
| 24 points | Mandatory 90-day license suspension + driver improvement class + probation for six months | Mandatory 90-day license suspension + driver improvement class + probation for six months |

For adults, the accumulation of eight demerit points in 12 months or 12 points in 24 months results in an advisory letter from the DMV. The accumulation of 12 demerit points within 12 months or 18 points in 24 months results in a mandatory driver improvement class. The driver improvement program must be completed within 90 days, or the license will be suspended.

After completing the mandatory driver improvement course, the driver is then placed on DMV probation for six months. After the probation is over, the driver is placed on an 18-month control period. If the driver receives another violation while on the control period, the driver reverts back to the six-month probationary period.

The accumulation of 18 points in 12 months or 24 points in 24 months results in a mandatory 90-day license suspension. Once that period has expired, the offender must complete a driver improvement class before his license can be restored. After restoration, the driver will be on probation for six months followed by an 18-month control period.

If the driver is convicted of a traffic offense while on DMV probation, his license will be suspended. The driver's license will be suspended for 45 days for a three-point violation, 60 days for a four-point violation, and 90 days for a six-point violation. Once that individual finishes the suspension period, he will be placed on probation for an additional six months followed by 18-month control period.

Anyone charged with reckless driving or any traffic violation should check to see whether the DMV may restrict their privilege to drive.

# Chapter 3:
## "How Do They Know If I Was Speeding?"
### How the Police Catch Speeders

Law enforcement can use a wide range of evidence to prove a driver was speeding. Each tool uses slightly different science, and each has its own weaknesses. The following chapter discusses the common ways that the police catch drivers speeding, as well as critical information about those methods' strengths and, more importantly, their weaknesses.

## Tracking History

A "tracking history" is an essential part of the speed enforcement process no matter what type of speed measuring device an officer is using. A tracking history is a series of observations that an officer makes in order to guarantee that the speed measurement was accurate. A proper tracking history has basically three requirements: 1) the officer makes a visual estimation of speed before measuring the target vehicle's speed; 2) the officer measures the speed of the vehicle continuously and as long as it is both reasonable and safe; 3) the officer checks for potential sources of error.

## LiDAR (Laser)

Light Detection and Ranging (LiDAR) is the newest method of measuring a driver's speed. LiDAR guns, or "Laser guns" are hand held devices that police officers point at cars to measure the car's speed.

LiDAR guns measure speed by using a "time-in-flight" method. The machine shoots invisible, infrared laser beams one at a time at a rate of about 120 to 238 beams per second for a least a .3 seconds burst. The machine then tracks the time it takes each of the beams to bounce back. The machine simply measures how much time each beam spent "in flight" and multiplies the time by the speed of light (983,571,072 feet per second) and divides the product by two to calculate the distance between the gun and the target. Each pulse takes a distance measurement, so the Lidar gun measures the distance between it and the target 120 to 238 times per second.

The machine then measures the change in distance during this distance measuring process and determines the speed of the target. For example, if during a .3 second burst the target started out at 546 feet and ended at 510 feet away, then the machine knows the object traveled 36 feet in .3 seconds. This equals 120 feet per second or 81.8 miles per hour.

There are many different types of LiDAR units that may be used by Virginia law enforcement officers; however, any LiDAR device used by law enforcement must be approved by the Virginia Division of Purchase and Supply. The most common LiDAR units used in Virginia are the Pro Laser III and the Pro Lite +. Both machines are manufactured by Kustom Signals. Both machines are required to measure speed within plus or minus one mph in order to be used as evidence in court.

**Lidar Range**
The theoretical range of a handheld LiDAR device is well over 2000 feet (approximately one-third of a mile). However, the effective range on LiDAR is limited by several things including the beam width in relationship to the targets size, the reflective quality of the target, atmospheric conditions, and the steadiness of the operator's hand. Range can also be limited when the officer is sending the beam through glass (such as the windshield).

The width of LiDAR's infrared beam is usually about .003% of the distance from the gun. Therefore, if a police officer measures a car that is 1,000 feet away, the car is being struck be an infrared circle that is 36 inches in diameter. As the range becomes greater, the beam diameter gets bigger. As the diameter gets bigger, it becomes more and more difficult to measure only one target's speed at a time and thus range suffers.

Most LiDAR devices will not produce a measurement if a significant portion of the beam produces multiple distance readings simultaneously (e.g. half the beam is striking a car and half is over-shooting and striking an object behind the car).

Generally speaking, the range of a LiDAR device is limited by the operator not the machine. An officer will have trouble continuously holding the beam completely on a moving vehicle that is more than 900 feet away and will have a hard time even identifying the make and model of a vehicle in day light if it is more than 800 feet away. While it is possible to get a measurement beyond these distances, it is much harder for the officer to obtain a legitimate tracking history of the target vehicle in order to guarantee the accuracy of the readings. For this reason some jurisdictions outside of Virginia have created rules against using LiDAR beyond 1000 feet.

In order for LiDar to work accurately, a certain percentage of the infrared beams emitted from the device must bounce back. If the beam is not pointed at something that reflects light well or if the object is not perpendicular to the device, then the portion of the beams that bounces back will be reduced. It will take longer to acquire a reading and the effective range will be reduced. Under ideal conditions it usually takes only .3 seconds for the LiDAR machine to produce a speed reading but the time it takes to acquire a reading gets longer as conditions worsen.

If not enough beams return to the gun, the LiDAR device will not produce a result. Consequently, the police are trained to aim the beam at a car's flat reflective surfaces, such as the license plate or headlights. Cars with hidden headlights or without a front license plate are harder to measure at distances beyond 700 feet in open air and more than 500 feet when through glass. Other conditions such as weather and the condition of the LiDAR lens can affect the range and speed of target acquisition.

**LiDAR Sweep Error**
Movement of the operators hand during the measurement process can cause erroneous speed measurements. If the police officer's hand moves during the measurement process, and the Lidar beam moves from one object to another, the difference in distance between the two objects may be read as if they were one object moving. This type of error is referred to as "sweep error." The greater the distance between the operator and the target the higher the likelihood of sweep error.

A common form of sweep error is when an officer shoots at the windshield of a vehicle and then moves the beam to the front license plate in order to get a stronger signal. The change in distance between the windshield and the license plate may result in a 5 to 7 mph increase in speed. This phenomenon can be demonstrated by sweeping the LiDAR beam rapidly from the windshield to the license plate on a parked vehicle. The stationary vehicle will produce a reading of 5 to 7 mph.

There are also reports of sweep error when an officer is measuring vehicles at a location where the road surface is somewhat perpendicular to the LiDAR operator. (e.g. shooting at hill or at a banking turn). Sweeping the LiDAR beam down the reflective road stripes along the road surface at these locations reportedly caused sweep errors of more than 90 mph. The faster the officers tracked the beam along the road the faster the reading on the LiDAR device.

Without a proper tracking history an officer cannot rule out the possibility of sweep error. Sweep error is more likely when the officer is taking "snap shot" speed measurements (i.e. taking a single speed measurement instead of continuously measuring the vehicle's speed over a period of several seconds). Sweep error is also hard to prevent at great distances where it is hard to visually estimate speed and where even slight tremors in the hands can result in rapid changes in the location of the beam.

**LiDAR Site Misalignment**
Law enforcement officers aim most LiDar devices with a heads-up display that contains crosshairs and a digital screen which can display speed, distance, and an estimated beam location. The heads-up display on any LiDAR device should never be magnified (most are not). This is because magnification makes the device more difficult to use at close ranges and distorts the officer's ability to visually estimate the vehicle's speed (an essential component of verifying that a LiDAR device is functioning correctly).

When an officer measures an object the digital heads-up display generates a red circle over the general location of where the beam struck the target. The crosshairs and this red circle are the only indication of where the very narrow (invisible) LiDAR beam is being directed.

As with gun sites, LiDAR sites can become inaccurate. Dropping or mishandling a LiDAR device can cause the heads-up display to aim inaccurately. If undetected or ignored, an error in the heads-up display can result in an officer attributing a speed measurement to the wrong driver (e.g pointing the gun at one car while measuring another car).

To prevent site misalignment, an officer should perform a vertical and horizontal site alignment test at the beginning and end of each shift. This will guarantee that the sites were functioning properly during the traffic enforcement period.

**LiDAR Calibration**
Every six months all LiDAR devices should be sent to a manufacture's laboratory to be tested for accuracy. Additionally, at the beginning and end of each shift the officer should test the LiDAR device in several ways.

First, the officer runs a "self-diagnosis". The officer will visually verify that all portions of the LCD screen are functioning and that the results of the self-diagnosis are positive. Then the officer measures a known distance with the LiDAR device and verifies that it is working accurately. Then the officer tests the heads-up display to guarantee that the sites are properly aligned. Proper calibration is essential to proper speed enforcement and failure to comply with these calibration requirements is a common way of defeating a LiDAR-based reckless driving case.

**Radar**

Radio Detection and Ranging (RADAR) technology is arguably the most common speed enforcement device in Virginia. Unlike LiDAR, which is pretty much "point and shoot," RADAR requires significant training and experience to obtain reliable results.

All RADAR units consist of a counting unit, the display, and at least one antenna. In handheld radar guns all three components are contained inside a single gun-shaped body. However, most RADAR units in Virginia are not handheld portable units. They are mounted inside police cruisers. The RADAR antennas are usually mounted on the front and back dashboards of police cruisers and the counting unit is usually mounted in the dashboard or center counsel. The display (if separate from the counting unit) is also on the dashboard.

In Virginia, modern police RADAR emits a continuous wave (instead of pulses). This continuous emission of microwaves spreads out at an angle of approximately 12 degrees for a distance of over 4,000 feet.

The microwaves continuously bounce off of all objects within the beam's path and return to the RADAR unit to be detected. Moving objects cause shifts in the returning microwaves frequency (known as Doppler shifts). The more distorted the return frequency, the higher the velocity of the target.

Objects moving towards the RADAR unit cause the frequency of the RADAR beam to rise while objects moving away cause the RADAR frequency to fall (this is the same phenomenon that makes the sound of an approaching car lower after it passes). Thus, by measuring the rise or fall of the Doppler frequency, the RADAR unit can calculate the relative speed and direction of any object within the scope of its beam.

When a police cruiser is moving, the RADAR unit is put into moving-mode and simply measures the cruiser's speed by measuring the relative speed of the ground in front of the cruiser. The unit's computer then adds or subtracts the cruiser's speed to the relative speed of the target object depending on whether the object is moving away from or towards the cruiser.

Some moving-mode RADAR units require the cruiser to be moving above a given minimum speed (usually around 20 mph) or require the object it is measuring to have more than a certain minimum relative speed (usually more than 3 mph) in order to give an accurate reading (i.e the cruiser and the target car cannot be going within 3 mph of each other).

Because moving RADAR requires the machine to accurately measure the speed of the cruiser and the speed of the target vehicle there is more potential for error. In order to verify the accuracy of moving RADAR, an officer must verify the RADAR's perceived ground speed against a calibrated speedometer at the time of measurement while simultaneously estimating the target vehicle's speed. A proper tracking history is very important.

**Target Identification Error**
The biggest problem with any RADAR unit is that it detects and measures any and all objects in the beam's path but only displays one or two speed results per antenna (depending on the make, model, and operating mode). The RADAR unit will display only the speed of the strongest signal it receives and/or the fastest speed it receives.

The strength of the signal has to do with the target vehicle's size, distance, material make-up and the target vehicle's location within the RADAR beam.

After a RADAR unit displays the speed of an object, it is up to the police officer to use his/her judgment in deciding which of the objects around the cruiser is responsible for the number on the RADAR's display.

In order to avoid target identification error, an officer should:

1) Visually estimate the target vehicle's speed prior to the vehicle entering the RADAR beam.
2) Note the change in the RADAR's readings when the vehicle enters the beams,
3) Verify that his/ her visual estimation and RADAR readings are reasonably similar,
4) Observe the vehicles readings during its entire duration within the beam,
5) Listen for a continuous high audio signal from the RADAR (a sign that the signal is not due to radio frequency interference or harmonic signal interference)
6) Note a corresponding change in readings when the vehicle exits the beam.

A proper tracking history, as defined above, is essential to guaranteeing that the officer has associated the right car with the right RADAR readings.

**Error From Rapid Changes in Speed**
Under ideal conditions, the accuracy of RADAR is about plus or minus one mph in stationary mode and plus or minus two mph in moving mode. However, several phenomena can cause the RADAR to give false readings (depending on the make and model of the RADAR unit).

Accelerating or decelerating more than one mph every .1 to 2.0 seconds can cause older RADAR units to be unable to track an object. This same weakness can affect the RADAR's ability to track the cruiser's ground speed. If either the police cruiser or the target car are significantly accelerating or decelerating, the RADAR may have trouble tracking the speed accurately. A proper tracking history will help expose this error.

**Harmonic Errors**
Harmonics can cause substantial false speed readings. Large targets (like trucks), reflective road signs close to the RADAR or large groups of targets (crowded traffic) can create echoes when a RADAR wave strikes the target vehicle and bounces off a nearby object(s) before returning to the RADAR unit. When the signal bounces off multiple moving objects, the frequency returns to the unit excessively distorted and generates an erroneous speed reading.

**Auto Locking**
The RADAR auto lock feature can also cause problems. Certain older units are designed to display no speed or various speeds until it tracks an object that is traveling above a certain mph limit. When the RADAR unit detects something going above the auto lock mph limit, an alarm sounds and the machine will not display anything but the speed of the target vehicle at the time it locked until it is reset.

This feature is problematic because a fluke signal that causes a high reading for only a split second will trigger the auto lock and any driver appearing to speed nearby will be blamed. Auto lock makes a proper tracking history impossible.

Many law enforcement agencies around the country have banned the use of this function. Devices that automatically lock as their default setting are not approved for use in Virginia. In Virginia, most speed measuring devices will manually lock after the officer hits a button. Manually locking a speed measuring device prior to establishing a complete tracking history is not much better than auto locking.

**Radio Frequency Interference**
Radio frequency interference (RFI) caused by substations, high power antennas, and the many two-way radios found in police cruisers can also cause random readings. Motion sensors, garage door openers, and obstruction detectors on heavy equipment and on the rear of some vehicles can also cause erroneous readings. The electrical equipment in the cruiser and along the highways can also generate false signals that may result in short, temporary, false speed results.

Radio frequency interference usually comes in to play only when either 1) the officer has set up a speed trap next to a strong RFI source (e.g. under power lines, etc.); 2) When the officer's RADAR unit power source has been wired using wires without RFI shielding or 3) When the RADAR unit's antenna wiring is bundled too closely to wires carrying RFI sources (e.g. a stereo power source, CB radio power source, antenna, etc.). Proper mounting and a proper tracking history will usually allow an officer to prevent RFI interference.

**Improper RADAR Antenna Mounting**
The moving blades of a cruiser's AC or heater fan can produce a RADAR signal of about approximately 15 to 45 mph. This is because most RADAR units' antennas are mounted on the dashboard near fan vents.

An officer's antenna should be securely fastened to the dashboard and should never be pointing across the RADAR's counting unit or across fan vents. Fan vents or the counting unit can cause "ghost readings", especially when there are no other stronger signals around.

Proper mounting and proper tracking history will help identify false readings caused by these types of error. An officer should also test for these errors by pointing the antennas along a deserted road, turning on the fan and turning up the RADAR's sensitivity. If a false signal is produced the mountings should be examined.

## Weather Error

Weather conditions such as precipitation and humidity can affect the range of RADAR and produce sporadic false readings. This is particularly likely when there is water, ice, or snow covering the road and the officer is operating the RADAR in moving mode. For this and other reasons, the Virginia State Police are trained not to operate RADAR when it is raining or snowing. As always, a proper tracking history is essential to prevent this error.

## RADAR Calibration

At the beginning and end of each shift, an officer is trained to calibrate their RADAR device. The device is calibrated by using tuning forks. The tuning forks are calibrated every six months to produce a frequency that is equal to the Doppler frequency of a vehicle moving at a specific speed (usually 35 or 65 mph).

The officer places the unit in test mode and strikes the tuning fork and places it inches away from the RADAR antenna. The officer then verifies that the RADAR device is producing a speed measurement that is within one mph of the tuning fork's calibrated speed.

If the officer is using the RADAR in moving mode then the officer must use both tuning forks simultaneously and then separately to perform the calibrations. Each device should be assigned its own specific set of tuning forks. Because different devices may use different RADAR frequencies, the tuning forks from different devices may not be interchangeable.

Every six months, the officers are required to have their tuning forks calibrated for accuracy. This is done at private and government laboratories here in Virginia. Each tuning fork must be accurate to within one mph and the RADAR unit must agree with the tuning fork to within one mph in stationary mode and two mph in moving mode. Consequently, the tolerance for a RADAR unit is two mph when in stationary mode and three mph in moving mode.

**Pacing**

Pacing is the simplest and most low-tech way of measuring speed. The police officer simply keeps pace with the target car. The officer then testifies that he was keeping a steady distance from the target car and states the speed on his speedometer at that time.

What many drivers do not understand is that an officer can pace a target car that is in front, to the side, or behind a police cruiser. Some officers will even pace a car that is on a highway while the police cruiser is on a parallel access road. Typically, the officer tailgates a target car in the same lane or one lane to the right.

Sometimes, when a car pulls up behind a police cruiser, the officer will gradually speed up to see how fast the driver behind is willing to go. After baiting the driver into speeding, the officer will pull the driver over.

In order to use pacing in court, a police officer must have had the car's speedometer calibrated recently (usually within six months before the offense date). Speedometer calibrations are done either by testing the cruiser's speedometer against a dashboard mounted

RADAR unit's measured ground speed or by using a dynamometer.

VASCAR, is an electronic stop watch system that reads the speedometer of the cruiser and calculates the distance between a moving vehicle and the police cruiser at two points. This allows the officer to pace at greater distances from a target vehicle and allows an officer to pace a vehicle that is traveling in an opposite direction. To be used at trial, the VASCAR system and the speedometer must have been calibrated within the last six months and the VASCAR system must be physically attached to the cruiser's speedometer cable.

Common pacing errors come from the officer not pacing for a sufficient amount of time, the officer speeding up to catch up with a target vehicle and then not decelerating completely prior to beginning the pace, attempting to pace a car that is accelerating or decelerating, attempting to pace a car that is changing lanes or separated by other traffic, or pacing from too far away.

If the officer is pacing from a different lane than the target vehicle, the officer cannot get an accurate reading on a curve. The cruiser will need to driver faster to keep up with the target car if it is on the outside of a curve or drive slower if it is on the inside. If you were paced on a curve and the officer was not directly behind you, tell your attorney immediately.

# Chapter 4:
## "Do I Have a Chance?"
### Yes! Why Drivers Should Never Assume They Will be Found Guilty

**Even If You Are Guilty, You Can Still Argue For a Reduced Punishment**

Even if you are guilty and even if the police can prove it, you still have a chance. Either through persuasion or by law, the results of a reckless driving charge are never a foregone conclusion.

There is a wide spectrum of punishments and alternative charges besides reckless driving. This means there is a lot of room for a prosecutor and defense attorney to negotiate even when there is no doubt to the driver's guilt. The biggest mistake a driver can make is to assume that there is nothing he or she can do.

In order to take advantage of this opportunity to negotiate, it is vitally essential to hire an attorney. Some prosecutors and some jurisdictions will not give unrepresented drivers the opportunity to meet before trial. Even in jurisdictions where citizens can talk to the prosecuting attorneys, an experienced attorney will walk into the negotiations knowing the prosecution and knowing which arguments matter to that prosecutor.

In each jurisdiction, different people will be the decision maker in your case. Some jurisdictions do not assign prosecutors to reckless driving cases while other jurisdictions do. Sometimes, the police officer acts as the prosecutor; other times the driver deals directly with the judge. Many unrepresented drivers never get the chance to negotiate a plea because by the time they figure out the process their opportunity to negotiate is gone.

**You Never Know When the Police or Prosecution Are Going to Make a Mistake**

Because the burden is on the government to prove the charges against you, there are many opportunities for a simple mistake to benefit your case.

To prove a driver's speed, the law enforcement officer must (among other things) prove that the equipment used to measure your speed was calibrated recently. They must prove that their equipment was used correctly and that the car they measured was the car they pulled over. The officer must bring proof of this to court and have that proof in the proper format.

The court will usually not require an officer to produce any evidence that their equipment was accurate unless the defense attorney has made the proper challenges according to Virginia's rules of evidence.

For other types of reckless driving, there are unique issues that may arise (such as whether the school bus was equipped with warning devices as required by Va. Code section 46.2-1090 or whether the witnesses are properly subpoenaed).

Each day, the courts throw out dozens of cases because the police or prosecution fails to prove these things and the defense attorney knew how to take advantage of the mistake.

**Just Because the Police Say You Were Driving Recklessly Does Not Mean that You Were**

In speed cases, do not let the fancy electronics fool you into believing that the police caught you speeding. Speed measuring devices break, wear down, and are only as good as the operator using them. For a detailed explanation of speed measuring devices and their potential errors review chapter 3.

Officers erroneously charge innocent people more frequently in reckless driving cases that involve accidents. In most accident cases, the officer has no first-hand knowledge about what happened. The officer is dependent on witnesses to know what happened. Witnesses can lie, make mistakes, or officers can issue citations without fully understanding what the witnesses have to say (especially when there is a language barrier).

Officers make mistakes more often in cases that involve unusual forms of reckless driving. Even though there are over 14 different types of reckless driving in Virginia, 95% of the reckless driving tickets are written for 46.2-862 (Speeding) and 46.2-852 (Reckless Generally). Some officers can go years without ever having to write a ticket for one of the other types of reckless driving. Consequently officers can make mistakes when they write tickets for one of these more unusual types of reckless driving. For example, officers sometimes forget that a person has to have had warning that their vehicle was broken before they can be convicted of 46.2-853 (Improper control).

It is also important to remember that many forms of reckless driving are extremely subjective. What an officer considers "reckless" a judge may not consider reckless. It takes an intimate knowledge of the case law and ample experience with the local judges before a person can accurately determine whether certain behavior will be considered reckless. That is where an experienced reckless driving attorney is extremely helpful.

# Chapter 5:
## "Do I Really Need an Attorney?"
Top Ten Reasons to Hire an Attorney

Every time I am in court, I see dozens of people show up at trial and get burned because they did not have an attorney. No one likes spending money on an attorney, but your reckless driving trial is not the time to be cheap. A conviction may cost you a lot more than you expected. Here are ten reasons why anyone charged with reckless driving should hire the best attorney he can afford.

**1. Reckless Driving Is a Serious Class 1 Misdemeanor, NOT a Traffic Ticket**

If you have been accused of reckless driving, you have been accused of committing a crime. Reckless driving is a class 1 misdemeanor, which is the most serious type of misdemeanor in Virginia. Other class 1 misdemeanors include assault and battery, DUI, possession of a concealed weapon, and petty larceny.

Reckless driving can result in up to 12 months in jail and a six-month suspension of your driver's license (six months to two years for racing). A reckless driving conviction can cost a driver their job if they drive for work, and it can jeopardize their security clearance.

A driver may be forced to disclose their conviction on background checks, job applications, and applications for higher education. Reckless driving may also prevent a driver from enlisting in the military or becoming an attorney.

A reckless driving conviction cannot be expunged. Once you have been convicted of reckless driving, it is on your criminal record forever. Expungements are only available if the charges are dismissed or dropped.

Reckless driving is a six-demerit-point violation in Virginia and remains on one's driving record for eleven years. If a driver has a less than perfect driving record, he may be in jeopardy of having his license revoked by the DMV or being placed on driving probation. Probation will be automatic for minors who are convicted of reckless driving.

Having a reckless driving conviction on your driving record also means that police will be less likely to give you warnings for simple traffic violations, and that prosecutors and judges will be even harsher on you in future.

## 2. Good Attorneys Pay for Themselves

A single reckless driving charge can cost a driver thousands of dollars in fines, court costs, insurance premiums, and DMV fees. The maximum fine for a reckless driving charge is $2,500. Court costs are about $80 and DMV license reinstatement fees are another $145, but the biggest expense is the insurance premiums. Some insurance providers will double insurance premiums for a first-time reckless driving conviction. Some insurance providers treat reckless driving convictions the same as drunk driving. These insurance hikes usually last three years, and can cost a driver more than $1,500.

The people most likely to experience an insurance hike are the very best drivers who are paying very little because of their unblemished record. This is especially likely if they are covered by a preferred provider or are receiving a good driver discount. The lower your premiums are now, the more you have to lose from a reckless driving conviction.

If a driver already has a very bad record they may dropped by their insurance provider and required to get high-risk driver insurance (SR-22 insurance).

Because of the extreme insurance premiums, many employers will not hire a person with a reckless driving conviction if the job involves driving a company vehicle.

If you are in jeopardy of an insurance hike or if a reckless driving charge could affect your employment opportunities, a good reckless driving attorney can easily save you more money than they cost.

In some cases, drivers can save a lot of money by sending an attorney to court in their place. For drivers who do not live in Virginia or who cannot afford to take off work to go to court, hiring an attorney may cost less than appearing in court.

When you total up the lower fines, the lower insurance effects, the time and travel saved, etc., a good attorney can usually save a driver more than they cost.

## 3. You May Not Have to Show up at Trial If You Have an Attorney

When a driver is charged with reckless driving, the police officer has a choice to arrest the driver and take him immediately to jail or to issue a summons ordering him to appear in court. The yellow piece of paper that you signed, which looks exactly like a traffic ticket, is called the Virginia Uniform Summons.

In some cases, a defendant who was issued a Virginia Uniform Summons may send an attorney to appear on his behalf instead of coming to court himself. The attorney can either try the case or negotiate a plea without the defendant being present.

This ability can be very convenient for the many out-of-state drivers charged in Virginia or for any other drivers who cannot come to court.

**4. Lone Defendants Are Treated Differently Than Those With Attorneys**

Some jurisdictions do not provide unrepresented defendants with the opportunity to negotiate a plea with a prosecutor. Not having an opportunity to negotiate a plea is a massive disadvantage. By having an opportunity to negotiate with a prosecutor, represented drivers double their opportunities to convince the court to show them leniency.

Besides negotiation opportunities, almost every jurisdiction gives represented defendants scheduling preference on the day of trial. This means that the judge calls your case only when your attorney is ready instead of whenever your file appears on the judge's desk. In some jurisdictions a driver without an attorney cannot be late to court, cannot step out to go to the bathroom, cannot go to check the parking meter for fear of their case being called while they are gone.

**5. The Day of Court Can Be Extremely Confusing and Chaotic Without an Attorney**

On a busy day in the Fairfax County courthouse there can be over thirty courtrooms operating at the same time with six courtrooms just for traffic cases. The judges assigned to traffic court have three and a half hours to complete 150-200 traffic cases. If they are lucky, they can finish in time to grab lunch before they begin the afternoon felony docket. That means that a single judge has an average of 60-84 seconds to complete each traffic case.

Things move fast in court. Judges, bailiffs, and prosecutors are often too busy doing their jobs to stop and help unrepresented defendants. Judges use legal slang in court and few people know what is going on if they do not have an attorney. Unrepresented defendants often just get ignored and convicted before they even realize that their trial is over.

One of the saddest things about being a defense attorney is sitting in court each day and watching dozens of unrepresented people come to court and just get mowed down by the system because they do not have an attorney.

### 6. The Learning Curve Is Brutal Without an Attorney

The judicial system is not forgiving. A defendant must submit his paperwork correctly and in a timely manner. If you do not make the right request to the right person, you will not get what you want.

Eighty percent of being an attorney involves knowing how the system works, and the vast majority of the court rules are not written down. Tradition, case law and etiquette govern much of what goes on in court.

By the time an unrepresented driver stands up before the judge, that driver has already lost many of the opportunities that could have made a difference in his case. Many times, the unrepresented driver spends hours preparing for his defense, only to be informed that his evidence is not in the right format or that he did not fill out the proper paperwork. The learning curve is brutal without an attorney.

## 7. You Never Know What Kind of Case You Have Until It Is Too Late

Some people do not get an attorney because they think there is nothing an attorney can do for them. Do not be fooled: reckless driving cases can be extremely complicated and difficult to prosecute. Read *Chapter 4: "Do I Have a Chance?"* to learn about the many different defenses to a reckless driving charge.

There is no reason to not at least talk to a reckless driving attorney and get a free consultation to learn what they can do for you.

## 8. Do Not Enter the Red-Tape Jungle Alone

How do I get a restricted driver's license? Where do I pay the court costs and fines? How do I arrange a payment plan for my court costs and fines? How do I get my license back? What happens if I am are sick and miss my court date? What do I do if I get a traffic ticket while on probation? How do I change my court date?

I could list a hundred questions people ask when they enter Virginia's judicial system. The sheer amount of paperwork and bureaucracy involved in a simple reckless driving case is staggering. Do not enter the red-tape jungle without a guide. You may never be seen again.

Red tape is not only frustrating and tedious; it can also get you arrested. One of the most important things a good attorney can do is make sure that you comply with your probation. Many serious reckless driving convictions (especially those at high speeds or that involve serious accidents) come with a lot of suspended jail time and fines. This suspension means that if you fail to comply with all the conditions of your probation, you risk going to jail and paying the extra fines.

I have seen plenty of drivers go to jail because they tried to take care of their probation requirements themselves and promptly got arrested for simple, little mistakes.

Make sure that you have an attorney that will walk you through the post-trial paperwork and not merely represent you at trial.

## 9. You Have Better Things to Do

Your attorney may be able to have the court waive your appearance in court. This means that your attorney can appear in court without you needing to be present. If you do not live near Fairfax County or if missing work is not an option, retaining an attorney may save you a lot of money and time.

Even if appearing in court is not a problem, drivers should ask themselves whether they want to spend the next few months dealing with their reckless driving charges or living their lives. Between work and family, the reckless driving defendant is also dealing with the possibility of losing his driver's license, going to jail, or even losing his job. Do you want to spend that time trying to figure out how the court system works as well?

Hiring a good attorney not only makes good financial and strategic sense, but it is an enormous emotional relief during a very stressful time. It can be invaluable to know that someone you trust is taking care of your case while you take care of the rest of your life.

## 10. You Probably Do Not Qualify for a Court Appointed Attorney.

Many people ask me about hiring their own attorney versus applying for a court-appointed attorney. In order to get a court appointed attorney your need to meet two requirements: 1) you need to be extremely poor and 2) you need to be in serious danger of going to jail.

Only the poor (or indigent) are provided with free attorneys. In order to be declared indigent in the Commonwealth of Virginia, you must make less than or equal to 125% of the Federal Poverty Line. The Federal Poverty Line is adjusted by how many people are in your family. The poverty line for one person is $9,800. The line for two people is $13,200, for three is $16,600, and for four is $20,000. Hence, if the defendant's family (of four) has an income of more than $25,000 ($20,000 x 1.25), then the defendant is too rich to get a court-appointed attorney. For most people, a court appointed attorney is not a possibility.

Even if you are poor enough to get a court appointed attorney, you cannot get one unless the prosecution is seeking a jail sentence. If a judge offers you a court appointed attorney that means you are likely going to jail if you are found guilty.

## Chapter 6:
## "How Do I Find a Good Reckless Driving Attorney?"
How to Spot a Bad Attorney and What to Look for in a Good One

### A Bad Contract Equals a Bad Lawyer

The attorney you hire is only as good as the contract you sign. The contract spells out what the attorney will and will not do for you. Some contracts end as soon as the trial is over and do not require the attorney to help you with any of the post-trial obligations you may have.

Make sure the attorney you hire will walk you through the complicated post-conviction processes and take your case to appeal if needed. Remember, it does not matter how good an attorney is if the contract does not require your attorney to help you.

### Do Not Base Your Decision Solely on Quantity of Experience

Some bad attorneys have been doing a terrible job for many years. And some of the best attorneys only take a very limited number of cases. Be cautious of hiring an attorney based solely on the number of years they have been practicing or the number of cases they have handled. To find quality experience, there is no substitute for having a meaningful discussion about your case with any attorney you are thinking about hiring.

Use the free consultation as an opportunity to discuss possible strategies and defenses in order to get to know an attorney.

## What is the Attorney's Area of Expertise?

Some attorneys are what we call "general practitioners." They do many types of legal work: divorces, lawsuits, wills, criminal defenses, adoptions, or whatever else pays the bills. Other attorneys limit their practice to one area of law, and other attorneys fall somewhere in between. Find out what percentage of the attorney's practice is spent on reckless driving or other traffic law issues.

## Who is Going to Handle Your Case at Trial?

At some law firms, the big name partners do the client interviews and the associates do the work. Make sure you know who is going to do your work, not just who is going to supervise the person doing your work. Many clients pay big bucks to an attorney who just outsources their case to an associate.

Interview all people who will be doing work on your case and read the contract carefully to determine whether it gives the specific name of who will be handling your case.

## Too Busy or Too Lazy

Most of the mistakes made by criminal defense attorneys happen because those attorneys are too busy, not because they are inexperienced or incompetent. Your attorney needs to have all the facts about the case and understand how the various consequences of a reckless driving conviction will affect you. There is no substitute for spending time talking with your attorney. If you do not feel like you have had enough time to talk, get another attorney.

Busy attorneys also tend to forget their place. An attorney is a counselor, not the client's babysitter. The attorney's job is to explain the options and consequences to the client and thus empower the client to make informed decisions. An attorney that is too busy does not have the time to communicate. Instead, the attorney wants to make all the decisions and have the client just come along for the ride. This situation is a formula for disaster: if your attorney wants to make decisions for you, get another attorney.

Because most of a reckless driving trial happens outside the courtroom, most of what an attorney does is done without anyone looking over his or her shoulder. If an attorney is too busy, there are plenty of places to cut corners without a client's knowledge. If you suspect that your attorney is a bit too busy, things are probably much worse than you realize. You should get another attorney.

**Does Your Lawyer Really Care About You?**

The second biggest complaint I hear from defendants is that their attorney does not care. Criminal defense can be an emotionally demanding profession, and some attorneys have become callused. They just stop caring. If you feel your attorney is not concerned enough about your problems, do not wait another day to hire another attorney. You need an attorney you know is going to fight for you 100%.

**Is Your Lawyer Detail Oriented**

When it comes to criminal defense, the devil is in the details. While most of the mistakes attorneys make come from being busy, the second biggest source of mistakes is not paying attention to details.

I saw this first-hand as a new attorney when I watched a driver go to jail for five days simply because his defense attorney did not notice a typo on the plea agreement. As the bailiff dragged the confused and terrified man to jail, the judge told the attorney that she should have read the agreement more carefully. You *do not want this to happen to you!*

Make sure that you hire someone who pays attention to details and is very thorough.

**Discount Attorneys Can Be Very Expensive**

Hire the best attorney you can afford. Cheaper attorneys need to serve more clients to make the same amount of money. Serving more clients means that they are busier and have less time to dedicate to your case.

While being less expensive does not always mean that an attorney is lower quality, be wary of any lawyer who main selling point is their low price. The most expensive attorney is the one who does not do their job right.

**Is Your Attorney Too Passive or Too Aggressive**

Before you go to trial, your attorney will have a chance to talk the prosecution into giving you what you want without a trial. Most reckless driving cases are resolved between the defense attorney and the prosecution without ever going to trial. Unlike trial, negotiations with the prosecutor are all about people skills.

Bad attorneys are often either too passive or too aggressive. Passive attorneys may give up too easily and just want to avoid going to trial. On the other hand, aggressive attorneys may make enemies out of the people who will be deciding your future. Judges and prosecutors have long memories.

The best attorneys are friendly, confident, and assertive. They can demand respect while treating others respectfully. If an attorney bad-mouths the judges and prosecutors, odds are that the judges and prosecution are bad-mouthing that attorney. You do not want to be the client of the attorney everyone hates.

**10 Things to Look for in an Attorney:**

1.  Offers a free consultation
2.  Can articulate well how he will defend you.
3.  Does mostly reckless driving cases
4.  Contract promises to help you with post-conviction programs and includes free appeals.
5.  Returns your phone calls and is easy to get a hold of
6.  Gets along well with the judges and prosecutors
7.  Listens carefully and answers all of your questions
8.  Empowers you to make your own decisions
9.  Organized and detail oriented
10. Cares about you and your case.

# Chapter 7:
## "What Do I Need to Do to Prepare for Trial?"
How to Get the Most out of Your Attorney

### Get an Attorney as Soon as Possible

If you receive a summons for reckless driving, get the best attorney you can afford *as soon as possible*! You are going to pay the same price for an attorney no matter when you hire one, so you might as well hire one sooner and get more service for your money.

A good attorney will also help you prepare for trial. For example, he or she can help you choose and complete the correct driving improvement program, check your DMV record for errors, and gather evidence.

### Proving Innocence and Mitigating The Punishment

There are two types of evidence: 1) evidence that proves innocence, and 2) mitigating evidence that suggests that you deserve a less severe sentence. Whether you are innocent or not, you need to gather both types of evidence. Once again, your attorney should help you with this process.

### Write Down Everything

As soon as you are ticketed, write down all the details that you can remember. In Virginia, the prosecution may not have to notify you or your defense attorney about the evidence it has against you before trial. Therefore, your attorney's most important source of information is you.

The most important details that you should write down are details of all the conversations you had with the police. What questions did they ask you? What did you say to them?

## Gathering Documents

Do not procrastinate gathering evidence. Any documents used in court should be originals or certified copies. A good attorney can help you gather evidence, so retain your attorney sooner rather than later.

Some of the documents you will want are your DMV records from all the states that have issued you a driver's license in the last five years. Defensive driving class diplomas or speedometer calibrations certificates may also be useful in your case.

Before taking any driving classes talk to a local reckless driving attorney. Taking the wrong class or taking the class at the wrong time could hurt your case and waste your time and money.

## Defensive Driving Classes

Attending certain defensive driving classes can restore up to five points to your Virginia driver's license and may encourage a judge or prosecutor to give you a more lenient sentence. However, there are many different types of driving classes. There are the VASAP aggressive driving classes, the Virginia DMV driver improvement classes, the AAA driving classes, and many other local driving classes. Contact a reckless driving attorney to find out which class is appropriate for your case.

In some jurisdictions the court may offer driver improvement programs as an alternative to conviction. However, if a driver takes a driving improvement class before trial, the driver may be disqualified from entering the program.

Before taking any driving classes talk to a local reckless driving attorney. Taking the wrong class or taking the class at the wrong time could disqualify you from some programs.

**Restitution**

If reckless driving results in an injury or destruction of property, the driver, under the supervision of his attorney, may want to pay restitution to the other party before trial in order to increase the likelihood of a reduced sentence. However, make sure you consult your attorney before making or discussing any restitution payments.

**Prepare for the Worst-Case Scenario**

Talk to your attorney and make sure that you are ready for the worst-case scenario on the day of trial. Do not drive yourself to the courthouse if there is any chance of a license suspension. If you are found guilty and either lose your license or are sentenced to jail, you cannot drive home.

Take the time before trial to get your finances in order so that you can pay any possible fines on time. Arrange to take time off work to go to court or to serve jail time. Talk to your attorney about the possibilities of the various sentences, and get your life in order in case of the worst-case scenario. Also, leave all valuables (cell phone, cash, watches, etc.) at home so you will not risk losing them at the court or in the jail's property room if you are sentenced to jail.

## Can I Get a Continuance?

Continuances are very important and limited in number. Continuances should never be wasted. Continuances can be used to discover what evidence the prosecution has against the driver. The attorney can show up on the day of trial, talk to the police and commonwealth attorney, and find out what evidence they have. Then the attorney can get a continuance in order to prepare a tailored defense.

Continuances may also be necessary to retain the attorney you want to hire. If the attorney you believe is the best for your case is not available on the day of your trial your attorney can get a continuance.

Being granted continuances may increase the odds that the court will grant the other side a continuance if it asks for one. If the police officer does not show up at trial, your attorney will ask for the case to be dismissed. However, if the court has already granted you several continuances, the court will be more inclined to grant the Commonwealth a continuance as well.

Do not put yourself in a position where you or your attorney will have to waste continuances. Find a quality reckless driving attorney immediately.

# Chapter 8:
## "What Is Going to Happen at Trial?"
### What to Expect on the Day of Trial

The typical judicial experience in Virginia varies wildly between jurisdictions. In Hampton, some judges moves so fast that drivers plead and are sentenced before they reach the front of the courtroom.

In Rockbridge County, the single courtroom may spend an entire day on less than 20 cases. However, a single judge in Fairfax County may have up to 200 cases to finish in three and a half hours.

Beyond the amount of cases, each jurisdiction has its own method of running the courts. Most courts begin the docket by getting the quick business out of the way: motions and unrepresented drivers pleading guilty. Larger courts almost always organize the cases by police officer, starting with the officers that have the fewest cases.

Usually, the courts will call out the names of people without attorneys, setting aside the defense attorneys' cases for last. It is always important to sit in the courtroom and listen for your name unless your attorney tells you otherwise.

## Negotiating Before the Trial

In some jurisdictions the prosecutors will not negotiate with unrepresented drivers. Often the negotiations go on in separate rooms while the court is calling and handling the cases of driver's without attorneys.

During the negotiation process, the defense attorney will get to hear the evidence against the client and start negotiations for a possible plea deal. Smaller jurisdictions may allow the defense attorneys to negotiate the plea before the trial date. In the larger jurisdictions, the prosecutors of misdemeanor cases almost always refuse to negotiate until the day of the trial because they are too busy to review the case before the day of the trial.

**What If I Am Late to Trial?**

Most traffic cases start between 9:00 – 11:00 a.m. Make sure you know the exact time and date of your case. Show up early. Failure to show up at trial may result in the judge trying and punishing you in your absence or issuing a bench warrant for your arrest. You do not want to have this happen to you so plan to arrive early and allow time for flat tires, traffic, or choked security lines.

**Sit and Watch Trials**

While your attorney waits to talk to prosecutors, sit in the courtroom and watch. Get an idea of how strict the judges and prosecutors are by watching other reckless driving and traffic cases. This will help you know whether the deal you are offered is a good deal or not.

**Plea Agreements**

After a defense attorney has had an opportunity to negotiate with the prosecution, the client will have an opportunity to either except or reject the terms of a plea deal. If the client accepts the terms of the plea, the defense attorney will present the plea agreement to the judge.

Plea agreements are *not* set in stone. After a guilty plea, a judge has the right to alter a plea deal if the judge wants to. Most plea agreements are just suggestions to the judge rather than a binding agreement. If a judge does alter the agreement, the defense attorney may ask to retract the guilty plea. If the judge does not retract the guilty plea, the defense attorney may appeal to the Circuit Court and retry the case. However, most judges rarely alter the plea agreements.

## Trial

If a client does not accept a plea agreement, he can still decide whether to plead guilty, not guilty, or no-contest. (In Virginia, there is usually no significant difference between pleading "guilty" and "no-contest.") The defendants pleading "not guilty" are usually the last people in the courtroom to be heard.

If a client pleads "guilty" or "no-contest," the court will only discuss what the sentence should be. If the client pleads "not guilty," the court will have a trial and discuss the issue of guilt. If the defendant is found guilty, the court will then discuss the sentence.

Reckless driving trials for unrepresented drivers are very quick and are typically rather informal. Usually, reckless driving trials with an attorney last about 20 to 30 minutes while trials without an attorney usually last about 60 to 80 seconds.

## Paying Fines and Costs

After the judge rules, a client who is found not guilty is free to go. If a client is found guilty, he will have to pay fines, fees, and court costs, and possibly register for a restricted license. A driver will have 15 days (from the date of trial or release from jail, whichever is later) to pay fines and costs unless they arrange a payment plan.

Most courts will allow a driver to set up a payment plan for a small additional price ($10 or more). Most courts will allow the driver to postpone payment for 90 days or less. A few courts have community service programs that they offer in exchange for waiving fines or costs. Most drivers will never hear about any of these options unless they have an attorney during the post-conviction process.

If a driver does not pay his court costs or comply with any court-ordered programs, he may lose his driver's license or may even be found in violation of the terms of his probation and be sent to jail. Your attorney can explain the payment process and verify that all of your payments have been received and processed by the court.

**What Do I Do if I Am Late or Miss My Trial Date?**

If you are going to be late or miss your trial date, call your attorney immediately. If you can contact your attorney *before* the judge issues a bench warrant, the attorney can ask the judge to either push your case to the very end of the docket or ask for a continuance and set a new trial date.

If a bench warrant is issued the attorney can file a motion to appear before a judge and ask the judge to remove the bench warrant. In this situation, the client must appear before the judge with his attorney. If the judge refuses to remove the warrant, the judge will set bail and the client will be arrested or issued a summons for the charge of failure to appear.

**What Happens if the Officer Does Not Show?**

If the officer or a witness does not show up to the trial, the case will either be continued to another date or dismissed. If the officer or witness is essential to the case and does not have an excuse for being absent, the judge may dismiss a reckless driving charge. However, depending on the jurisdiction and judge, an excused absence may result in a continuance unless the prosecution has already received too many continuances.

**Getting a Restricted License**

To get a restricted license, a driver who has had their license suspended by the court must be granted a restricted license by the judge. The driver will need to supply the court with the exact times and locations of all the places to which he regularly needs to drive (such as work, school, church, or medical treatment).

The judge may or may not grant the restricted license, or she may grant it under the conditions of the court's choosing. This can be problematic for clients who go to work at different times each day. It is essential to have an attorney available to help with this process, especially if you do not have the typical Monday through Friday, 9:00-to-5:00 job.

Once a driver gets his restricted license, the driver must carry it with him whenever he drives. Furthermore, he may only drive during the times stated on the license and between the locations approved on the license. Failure to do so may result in additional charges and more severe consequences, including jail time.

If a driver has a commercial driver's license (CDL), the Virginia DMV will not issue a restricted license even if the judge approves it. If you have a CDL, make sure that you inform your attorney.

## Suspended Sentences

In more serious reckless driving cases, a judge will often hand down a sentence with the majority of the jail time suspended. This kind of sentence is a form of "inactive probation." This means that the driver is on probation but does not have to report to a probation officer or do drug testing. Instead, the driver must pay all of his fines and costs, comply with any court ordered program, and avoid any other convictions or traffic offenses.

The judge will also declare a period of time for the probation to end. Typically, this period is one or two years. If the driver violates the conditions of his probation (for instance, gets another criminal conviction), he will appear before the judge to determine how much of the suspended sentence he will have to serve. Many judges typically require the entire suspended sentence be served. The suspended jail time will be in addition to the sentence for any subsequent convictions.

If you have any suspended sentences or probation from a previous conviction and you are ticketed again, immediately get an attorney and tell your attorney. Also, make sure you hire a reckless driving attorney who will walk you through the restricted driver's license registration process, so you can avoid accidentally failing to comply with your probation.

## When Can I Drive Again?

A driver who was found guilty of reckless driving may be forced to surrender his license to the bailiff of the court. He cannot drive until he has a restricted driver's license or has received his driver's license back from the DMV. A driver who has completed the suspension period cannot get his driver's license back until the suspension period has expired, he has paid the $125 DMV reinstatement fee, *and* he has been issued a driver's license from the DMV. If a driver has any concerns about whether he can get his license back, the driver should contact the Virginia DMV and request a "compliance summary." The summary will spell out all conditions necessary for the driver to get back his license.

**Expungements**

In Virginia, a driver's criminal record is permanent and public. A reckless driving conviction stays on your DMV record for eleven years but it stays on your criminal record forever. There is no way to expunge a reckless driving conviction in Virginia.

However, a driver may have the record of his arrest erased if the charges are dismissed, nolle prosequi ("nolle-prose"), or the driver is found "not guilty." If a driver wants to have his record expunged, he should contact a reckless driving attorney.

# Chapter 9:
## "Should I Appeal?"
### Pros and Cons of Appealing a Conviction

When a person is arrested for a misdemeanor in Virginia, he is tried in the General District Court (GDC) of the county, city, or town where the crime was committed. A conviction in the GDC can be appealed to the Circuit Court of Virginia within ten days.

If the defendant appeals to the Circuit Court, several things will happen. The GDC judge will issue a bond if the defendant was sentenced to jail, and the GDC's sentence and conviction will be completely erased.

The Circuit Court will then conduct a completely new trial (usually within one to three months). If the driver paid any fines or costs before appealing, the money will be credited towards any Circuit Court fines and costs or refunded after the Circuit Court trial. The court costs for appeals are about $150 more for non-jury trials and $550 per day for jury trials. A defendant has to pay these court fees if they are found guilty of any crime.

The Circuit Court (unlike the GDC) allows for jury trials; however, the decision to have a jury trial can have serious positive or negative effects on your trial. Consult an attorney about the pros and cons of having a jury trial.

During an appeal, the attorney will have another opportunity to negotiate with a prosecutor before trial. Unlike GDC, in Circuit Court, some appeals can be negotiated prior to the day of trial.

The decisions of the Circuit Court can be appealed to the Virginia Court of Appeals or the Supreme Court of Virginia. However, these courts can choose whether or not to hear those appeals, and they will only reverse decisions by the Circuit Court if the Circuit Court made a serious legal mistake. These reversals are much less common.

Every driver arrested for reckless driving should read his attorney-client contract carefully. Most attorneys charge extra for appealing a case to the Circuit Court. Before retaining an attorney, discuss the cost of an appeal.